SHORTHAND

*the text of this book is printed
on 100% recycled paper*

SHORTHAND

by John Comstock Evans
Author of *Touch Typewriting*

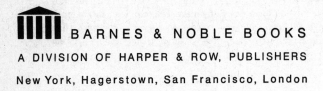 BARNES & NOBLE BOOKS

A DIVISION OF HARPER & ROW, PUBLISHERS

New York, Hagerstown, San Francisco, London

A PRELIMINARY STATEMENT

THIS HANDBOOK is designed to (a) meet the definite demand on the part of the everyday man and woman for a practical, self-teaching guide to shorthand, and (b) provide a text for classroom use. In both capacities it has proved eminently successful through five previous editions.

Shorthand, like longhand, is a means of representing speech by symbols. The shorthand symbols are briefer. The unique feature which makes EVANS SHORTHAND so easy to learn and to remember is that this system is related to longhand. Less effort is required to write EVANS SHORTHAND rapidly.

Speech consists of units of language which flow almost imperceptibly into one another. The units consist of either single letters of the alphabet or combinations of letters that are uttered with *single voice impulses*. The combinations are known as BLENDS, for their separate sounds blend to become each a SINGLE VOICE IMPULSE; and hence, in this system, blends—all the blends in the English language—are represented by single pen strokes.

"Thoroughness" should be the student's watchword and guiding principle in learning shorthand.

L. C. Catalogue Card Number : 46-3986

ISBN: 0-06-463225-3

79 80 12 11

Printed in the United States of America

FOREWORD

Evans Speed Shorthand is, in reality, VOICE WRITING, for its symbols are designed to represent the language UNITS of the SPEAKING VOICE, not solely the letters of the alphabet.

Simplicity, brevity, clarity, and legibility characterize this system of shorthand. It is a WHOLLY NEW SYSTEM—different in its basic conception, its structure, and its consociation with longhand. Although it is radically progressive, it has been proved to be just what it was intended to be—SUPERIOR in *ease of learning*, in *rapidity*, and, most of all, in *legibility*. And it has also been proved SUPERIOR by many years of office and reporting use. *It has been learned through home study by students in all sections of the United States.*

Its structural simplicity enables its writers to take difficult legal, medical, and scientific matter rapidly and accurately and to transcribe it correctly.

Evans Speed Shorthand is the only system having a complete alphabet. Distinctive characters are provided for *C, Q, W, X, Y,* and *Z*. Puzzling substitutes are thus eliminated.

Theory has been reduced to a minimum. Only a little more than one-third the usual theory is required. However, the system is complete, providing for useful short cuts and rational abbreviating processes. But nothing essential is omitted.

This system is easy to write because it is built around the circle. The circle is its symbol. Eighty per cent of the total fundamental characters are circles, curves, hooks, and loops—easily and readily formed.

It is rapid to write for the reasons stated above.

It is easy to read because *ninety per cent of its fundamental characters are definitely consociated with longhand.* A few are identical with longhand. *O* is a circle, *C* is like longhand, and *X* is a small cross. Vowels are identical with longhand or resemble the longhand closely. And, as vowels constitute approximately forty per cent of total characters, legibility is enhanced this much immediately by vowel forms.

Words are spelled as in longhand, silent letters (those not sounded) being omitted. Illustration: In other systems *quail* is spelled *K-W*-A-L. In this system it is spelled *QU-A-L* —just as it is in longhand (the *I* being omitted), and it is written with only two strokes as against four in other systems.

There is no reversal of longhand order of letters in shorthand outlines. Example: In other systems *wheel* is spelled *H-W*-E-L. In this system it is spelled *WH*-E-L, just as in longhand.

All characters are single strokes—the alphabet and blends. They are therefore shorter, easier, and quicker to write.

Blends are fully and logically developed for the first time in shorthand history. Every blend (consonant combination or coalescent) in the English language is represented by a single pen stroke. And there are more than twice as many blends as letters in the alphabet. Their importance is therefore apparent.

Time is saved on transcript since shorthand notes are read without hesitation.

High speed is quickly attainable because there is less theory to learn—about one-third that of traditional systems. The student's time is conserved for speed and transcription practice, and greater efficiency results.

This system is ideal for personal use, as there is little theory to learn; it is most rapid to write; and it is wholly legible.

JOHN COMSTOCK EVANS

TABLE OF CONTENTS

TABLE OF CONTENTS (Continued)

TABLE OF CONTENTS (Continued)

ALPHABET OF EVANS
SCIENTIFIC SPEED SHORTHAND

Vowels

I	E	O	OO	A	U	Y

Diphthongs

OI-OY   OU-OW

Consonants

Straight Lines

T	D	N	M	X

Left Curves   and   Right Curves

P	B	K	G	J	L	R	QU

Left Curves   or   Right Curves

S	Z	F	V
(or)	(or)	(or /	\ or /

Two Short Shallow Horizontal Curves

H	W

Hooks

Left or Right   Open Bottom

C	Y
(or)	

SHORTHAND

CHART No. 1

Dot and Circle Vowels

I	E	O	OO
.	°	○	○

What to Observe and Remember

I is a dot—the dot of longhand (small letter) script *i ı*.

E is a very small circle about the size of the initial or middle circle of longhand script capital *E ℰ* ° .

O is a circle—the size of longhand (small letter) script *o o*.

Double-*O* (*OO*) is twice the size of *o ○* .

Directions for Practice

Write the Dot and Circle vowels fifteen or twenty times in your notebook. Practice till you know them perfectly. Your practice work should look like this:

ı . . . . .

ℓ ° ° ° ° °

o ○ ○ ○ ○ ○

oo ○ ○ ○ ○ ○

CHART No. 2

Four Curved Consonants

H   W   L   R

What to Observe and Remember

H is a short shallow downward curve.

W is a short shallow upward curve.

L is a short *upward right curve. L* is the first stroke of longhand script *L* —to the crossing only.

R is an *upward right curve* (the first stroke of longhand script small letter *R* . It is a half longer than L.

Practice these characters till you know them.

Words for Practice

1. Circles are written inside curves.

he	hoe	woe	we	low	row	high	lie	rye

CHART No. 3

Four Straight Line Consonants
T   D   N   M

2. *T and D are written downward*—the same as the straight strokes in longhand script *T t* and *D d* . *D* is twice as long as *T*, the same length as the straight stroke in script small letter *D d*.

N and M are horizontal strokes. M is twice as long as N.

How to Practice

Write each letter in your notebook fifteen or twenty times or until you know it perfectly. *Pronounce aloud or silently as you write.*

Words for Practice

me knee no know mow moo night might meat neat

hit hid hide lid ride little riddle lee roll row

Observe: 1. When a circle is attached to a straight line it is written clockwise—in the direction in which the hands of a clock move.

2. Between two straight lines that form an angle, the circle is written outside the angle.

meet   need

Unit 2
Blends
Definition and Examples

3. When two or more consonants occur together in a word and they are spoken with a single or prolonged voice impulse, a coalescent or "blending" sound results, and the blended sound —voice UNIT— is represented by a single pen stroke to secure brevity. Examples:

SH   CH   ST

4. *SH* and *CH* are written downward. *CH* is twice as long as *SH*. They are vertical strokes. *ST* is a shallow downward curve twice the length of *H*. Practice the blends till you know them.

Words for Practice

shy		stone	
shine		stem	
chin		steam	
chime		lost	
din		roast	
dine		rest	
dim		stole	
dime		steal	
sty		meadow	
list		lime	
wrist		ream	
host		wren	
east		room	

The R Blend

5. Fourteen consonants and blends are followed by *R* and coalesce with it. These blends are indicated by SUPERSCRIPT— that is, BY WRITING THE CONSONANT OR BLEND PRECEDING *R* SLIGHTLY HIGHER THAN ITS USUAL PLACE TO ADD *R*. The usual place is on the writing line or *the line*.

Superscript Illustrated

tea   tree   teat   treat   Ted   tread   tot   trot   trod

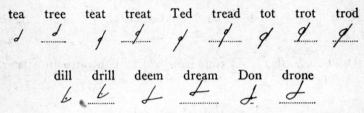

dill   drill   deem   dream   Don   drone

Where to Place Dot I

6. Write the dot:
(a) *Over angles of upward tendency:*
light   right   ride   lid   little   riddle   night   middle

(b) *In the vertex of other angles:*
shine   chime   chin   dime   dim   tin   din   dine   rim

(c) *Immediately before consonants that follow:*
isle   aisle   ill   ire   idle   eider   itch   immodest

(d) *Immediately after a preceding consonant:*
tie   die   dye   lie   rye   high   sty   nigh   my   shy

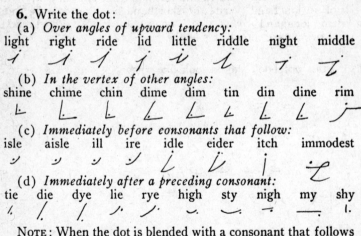

NOTE: When the dot is blended with a consonant that follows it, the word is divided to express *I*. For convenience of description we say the "pen lift" is *I*.

nine   mine   tight   tide   *tidy   dido   ditty   title

---

*Y as a vowel has the sound of short *I*.

Short L and Y

7. For convenience *L* is frequently represented by a very short shallow downward curve—half the length of *H* ⌣ . Short *L* is generally used after horizontal strokes and is frequently used after downward left curves as illustrated on page 23. Short *L* sometimes represents the blend *LT* at the end of a word as shown on page 40.

heel	hill	mile	knell	kneel	meal	mill	hole

The use of *Y* as a consonant will be illustrated in a later lesson.

How to Practice

8. Write each word in the left-hand margin of your notebook in longhand. Write the shorthand five times at the right of the longhand. SPELL EACH WORD EACH TIME YOU WRITE IT, and pronounce aloud or silently.

Your notebook should look like this:

he

we

hoe

low

high

row

lie

rye

Unit 3

Vowel Sounds

9. Since shorthand is the representation of the speaking voice, or the recording of spoken language by means of adopted symbols to represent VOICE UNITS, *it is most important that the student pronounce words correctly,* that he enunciate distinctly, and that he learn exactly the sounds of vowels, consonants, and blends.

The student should pronounce each word and each *vowel sound* aloud several times.

Dot and Circle vowels have two sounds each—short and long as illustrated below:

Short *I* as in	hit	lit	nit
Long *I* as in	night	might	light
Short *E* as in	net	met	hem
Long *E* as in	me	meet	meal
Short *O* as in	on	hot	tot
Long *O* as in	own	home	note
Short *OO* as in	hood	wool	stood
Long *OO* as in	moon	room	stool

After practicing the above sounds the student should write each word five times in his notebook, spelling the word as he writes and finally pronouncing the word aloud after writing it.

The sounds of *A, U,* and *Y* are illustrated on page 15, but they should not be studied until that page is reached.

Unit 4

Words for Practice

Write each word five times

hot		odd	
hod		ode	
heat		ore	
head		no	
mean		know	
moan		mow	
known		dough	
noon		row	
moon		team	
meet		ream	
metal		hem	
meter		lemon	
*need		toll	
needle		dole	
moat		hole	
mode		tile	
remote		dial	
remodel		loam	
†moment		room	

---

*A circle is written outside an angle.
†The suffix *ment* is represented by *M*.

Unit 5

Speed Graphs

Origin and Importance

10. The letters of the shorthand alphabet have word values. For example: *T* represents "it" and "to"; *N* represents "in" and "not"; *M* represents "am" and "more" etc.

Speed Graphs are usually a part of the word they represent; hence, they are easily learned and remembered.

Speed Graphs are used for brevity and speed. Their name indicates the latter purpose. *They must be committed and remembered.* The student failing to do this will pay dearly for his neglect later.

Practice each Speed Graph in your notebook twenty times or until you know it perfectly.

it, to	shall, ship
had	short
her, hear, here	change
do do not	charge
in, not	church
am, more	*I
the in the	who
this	a, an
is, his or	if
well, will	street, saint
are, air	you, your-s
were	year

---

*"I" is written *above* the line, "a" and "an" are *on* the line, "if" is *below* the line.

Speed Groups

11. Speed Groups are formed by joining words, usually Speed Graphs or Speed Graphs and other words. Their purpose is to save time and increase speed.

I am	I will	I do	I had	he had	he will	she will

1.

2.

it will	you will	you are	we will	we are—are not

1.

2.

he will not	I had not	I will not	we shall—shall not

1.

2.

to you	do you	will you	are you	with you	we do

1.

2.

who will	who are	who will not	who are not	we *were

1.

2.

---

*At the end of a group *W* may represent "were."

Unit 6

Sentences to Be Read and Practiced

(a) [shorthand symbols]*

1.

2.

(b) [shorthand symbols]

1.

2.

(c) [shorthand symbols]

1.

2.

(d) [shorthand symbols]

1.

2.

---

*Punctuation:

Period _____	Dash ___/___
Quotation marks " "	Paragraph ending ✕
Parentheses ( )	Proper noun_(tick beneath
Question mark (	word)

Sentences to Be Written

(a) I trod on a nettle.

1.

2.

(b) He will trim the willow tree.

1.

2.

(c) Don will not meddle with the hot metal.

1.

2.

(d)   The drone will not know Rome or room.

1.

2.

(e) Will you write change, charge, church, shell, ship, short, he, she, her, hear, it?

1.

2.

CHART No. 4

Left Curve Consonants

P	B	K	G	J

12. The left curves *P* and *B* are written *downward*. *P* is half as long as *B*. They are slightly slanted.

K, *G*, and *J* are written *upward* at a considerable slant.

K is the left curve upward stroke in script

G is the finishing stroke of script capital

J is the finishing stroke of script

Practice these consonants in your note book till you know them perfectly. Pronounce as you write.

Words For Practice

pie buy Poe beau pea bee kit kite pot go Joe

CONSONANT C   C or ɔ

13. The left hook *C* is like script *C* except the finishing stroke is shortened. *C* is also written as a right hook to form better joinings in certain cases.

Words For Practice

cot coat comb cod cede cite ceiling cob city

CHART No. 5

Angle and Hook Vowels

ANGLE A   HOOK A   HOOK U   HOOK Y

14. Any angle may represent *A*. Angle *A* is derived from the top part of longhand print capital *A* — the angle only. *U* is a hook open at the top just like the hook part of script *u*.

Angle A Illustrated

aim may tame mate dame made maid late lad raid

pan ban bane pain sham chain ran lane hat rat

cat cake came cane pack back Kate gate Japan

Write each word five times. Spell and pronounce as you write.

Two Functions of Hook A

15. Hook *A* is used to form more facile joinings in a few instances; and to distinguish the broad sound of *A* when necessary to do so.

gain game gamp Jane jamb Jan. khan Kansas

lay law ray raw Dan dawn lane lawn bale bawl

tale tall shale shawl gale gall mail maul hall

NOTE. Not every angle is *A*; but when *A* is necessary to the sense of the word, the angle represents *A*.

Unit 2

Sounds of the Vowels

A   U   Y

16. *A* has four sounds:

Long *A* as in   ate   ∕   Kate   ⌐∕   hate   ⌐∕   late   ∕

Short *A* as in   at   ∕   hat   ⌐∕   rat   ∕   cat   ⌐

Broad *A* as in   law   ∕   raw   ∕   tall   ∕   bawl   ⌐

Italian *A* as in   palm   ∠   calm   ⌐   *arm   ⊂   †task   ∕

U has two sounds:

Long *U* as in   mule   ⌐   mute   ⌐   tune   ↳   pew   ∠

Short *U* as in   hut   ⌐∕   mut   ⌐   rut   ∕   cut   ⌐

Y (in shorthand) has only one sound—that of:

Short *I* as in   lady   ⌐   tidy   ∕   shady   ∕

Nᴏᴛᴇ. In consociating Evans Scientific Speed Shorthand to longhand, *Y* is used as both a consonant and a vowel.

Y as a consonant illustrated: yoke   ⌐   yet   ⌐   yell   ∕

Although hook *A* and *Y* have the same form, no confusion results therefrom in actual practice.

A few words with different meanings have the same shorthand outline but the sense of the context will indicate what word should be used. Examples: hat   ⌐∕   hate   ⌐∕   at   ∕   ate   ∕

---

*AR is a deep narrow hook. See Art. 27.
†Speed Graph.

Unit 3

Diphthongs

OI-OY   OU-OW

17. *OI-OY* is a small loop; *OU-OW* is a large loop. Practice the loops. Pronounce aloud or silently.

Diphthongs Illustrated

bow	how	now	cow	allow	row	boy	joy	coy	*foil

The Blends CR, KR, GR, PR, BR Illustrated

crow	crate	cradle	krone	krona	grate	grade	grape

prate	braid	prim	brim	prowl	broad	pretty	brought

Words for Practice

pack	back	bag	badge	page	make	knack	wage	wedge

pick	brick	creek	crock	wig	big	brig	brain	prow

pad	paid	bad	wake	walk	take	talk	wait	wail	caw

rail	last	least	lost	lust	rest	roast	host	came

bell	bowl	towel	dowel	*grieve	grove	crape	grip

lock	rock	lodge	leg	ledge	kill	†lake	lack	wreck

leak	†trag	rug	rage	gage	rail	lair	hair	hail	hill

*F and V, page 23.

†Between curves in opposite directions *A* is understood when necessary to the sense of the word.

Unit 4
Speed Graphs

of ___o___, or ___O___

over ___O___

us _υ_ , use _ω_

as, has _ᴧ_

usual-ly _ω_

all _c_

cause _ɔ_

  because _ɔ_

if ___.___

answer _⌐_

into _)_   and _)_

put _(_

please ___(___

be, by _(_

  but, been _(_

hand, and _)_

special _∩_

capital-ol _ç_

can, come _ç_ or _ɔ_

car, care ___ç___ or ___ɔ___

call ___ç___ or ___ɔ___

credit-or _6_ _6_

jury _↑_

yes (es) _϶_ ·

good _↗_

great ___↗___

glad ___↙___

girl ___↗___

give-n _↗_

just _/_

judge _/↑_

gentlemen _∩_

him _•—_

yesterday _ᘔ_

any - my _↷_ ⟶ _↷_

many ⟶ _↷_

money ⟶ _•_

market ⟶ _↘_

mistake-n _—•_

was _↘_

today ___↗___

  data _/_

collect _6_

correct _6_

Speed Groups

to the	to come	to go	to give	to you	do you	of the

1.

2.

in the	on the	and you	and you are	may be	he is

1.

2.

if you will - not	if you are - not	I will be - put

1.

2.

has been	will be	will not be	if you will be	as is

1.

2.

he will	he will not be	we shall	we shall not be

1.

2.

with you	can you	into the	and the	it is	it is not

1.

2.

Unit 5

Sentences to Be Read and Practiced

(a) [shorthand notation]

1.

2.

(b) [shorthand notation]

1.

2.

(c) [shorthand notation]

1.

2.

(d) [shorthand notation]

1.

2.

(e) [shorthand notation]

1.

2.

(f) [shorthand notation]

1.

2.

(g) [shorthand notation]

1.

2.

---

*Clean. See page 24 *till.* [shorthand notation]

Sentences to Be Written

(a) John ate the ham and bun. Joe ate a big bun.

1.

2.

(b) The note will be due June 1. Will you pay it?

1.

2.

(c) Will you drill with us now? I shall drill with you.

1.

2.

(d) The gentlemen are in the hut in the dale.

1.

2.

(e) Will you go to the game with me if I pay your way?

1.

2.

(f) I shall be pleased to go to the game with you.

1.

2.

(g) Dan will not take the ticket at the gate, will he?

1.

2.

(h) Dale will greet us here today, and I shall greet him.

1.

2.

(i) I will meet the maid at the train today if she gets here.

1.

2.

(j) Don is making a dam in the stream by the mill.

1.

2.

The Blend TH

18. *TH* is a short shallow *right* or *left* curve written *upward.* ⌐⌐ ⌐   Speed Graphs: the ⌐ this ⌐ there ⌐

Illustrative Words

heath	hath	path	bath	both	breath	lath	wrath

thee	thin	these	theme	throw	thrive	threw	three

The Consonant X *x*

19. The consonant *X* is a cross like longhand. A short straight line through another consonant or vowel indicates *X.*

exist	exit	fix	mix	six	expect	expose	box	*vex

fox	examine	examination	Dixie	lax	wax	sax	ox

Past Tense, ING, INGS, INGLY

20. The past tense is usually expressed by a tick, but if the *TD* or *DD* is clearly enunciated, the blend stroke is used.

Ing is a dot; *ings* is a detached *s; ingly* is the *LY* stroke detached.

blushed	cashed	rated	going	knowingly	noted	earnings

SH represents any syllable pronounced *shun.*

notion	motion	lotion	vision	portion	mention	rotation

---

*See page 23 for *F* and *V.*

CHART No. 6

Right or Left Curves

Written Downward

S	Z	F	V
(or)	⌐ or ⌐	⌐ or /	⌐ or /

21. *S, Z, F,* and *V* are written downward as either right or left curves. The object of writing them either way is to form facile joinings. *An acute angle should be formed when possible.* Observe length and slant as above.

The Acute Angle Illustrated

sat fat vat fad sail fail vale fan vain fast vast

When to Use Short L

22. On page 6 we learned that short *L* is used after horizontal strokes. mail ⌐ mile ⌐ meal ⌐

heel ⌐ still ⌐ hole ⌐ Nile ⌐ steel ⌐

Short *L* is generally used after a downward left curve usually in unaccented syllables.

maple ripple people nipple gable label stable fable

NOTE: Regular *L* is used in the following words:
impel compel rebel expel complement compliment
implement

On page 40, line 6, we find short *L* is used to represent *LT* at the end of a word. pelt ⌐ belt ⌐ silt ⌐

colt ⌐ salt ⌐ fault ⌐ vault ⌐ volt ⌐

Unit 2

The L Blend When L Follows a Consonant

23. Fifteen consonants and blends are followed by *L* and coalesce with it. Hence, *L* blends are quite useful.

24. Writing a consonant or blend *subscript* (lower than its regular place) adds *L* to a curve and *EL* to a straight line. However there are two exceptions to this rule: Writing *R* and *V* subscript adds *EL*.

Initial consonants are written through the base line.

blow	blue	blot	plot	plate	blight	blame	black	plum

tell	deal	dell	shell	delight	real	relay	relish	reel

25. Medial consonants are frequently written subscript to add *L*. And, by dividing the word often *I* is expressed also.

whistle	thistle	missile	gristle	sizzle	fizzle	frizzle

complain	complete	implicit	explicit	inflame	reflect

or

26. Circles and hook are written inside of curves.

see	so	fee	foe	few	pew	beau	go	zeal	zero	we	he

Practice Words

race	rice	ice	chance	dance	nice	mice	council-sel

post	boast	*lack	lake	lag	rag	rug	rack	rig	lick

crack	cross	crease	crag	click	clove	cleave	clue	cry

---

*A is understood between reverse curves.

Unit 3

R Blend when R Follows a Vowel

27. *Enlarged hook A expresses AR* ∩ U ⊂ ⊃ This hook may also express *ER* at the end of a word when *E* and *R* blend. And, sometimes the same hook may express *R* only.

par bar jar garment arm mar art arch parch far Negress

meager eager paper baker sober Negro degree digress

28. *Cutting a circle or loop adds R.*

pour bore wore store gore core bower lore power

peer beer steer fear near mere rear shear cheer

29. *Writing final or medial I superscript adds R.*

tie tire die dire wire hire mire chirp fire stir

pyre buyer shy shire birch birth firth (TH Art. 18)

30. *Turning U on its side adds R.*

cure incur injure pure purr burr fur burn churn

Practice Words

rubber robber taper reaper leper fiber tuber arbor

train drain brain press stress breeze shriek prose

crack cross crane crag click clove clever stream

Place Comparisons

Superscript R Blends—Subscript L Blends

Compared with each other and with words having same outline but written in regular place.

fate	fight	fee
freight	fright	free
flat	flight	flee
bake	go	boat
break	grow	brought
black	glow	bloat
foe	fame	best
fro	frame	breast
flow	flame	blest
fees	feet	pun
freeze	fret	prune
fleas	fleet	plum
book	folk	fail
brook	frock	frail
block	flock	flail
gas	bush	cash
grass	brush	crash
glass	blush	clash

The SL Blend Illustrated

slate ___ sleet ___ slight ___ sled ___ sleep ___ slip ___ slide ___

slow ___ slope ___ slain ___ slam ___ slim ___ slice ___ slosh ___

LY and RY Blends

31. *LY, LI, LEY, ALY,* and *ILY* are expressed by W at the end of a word. *RY* and *RI* are expressed by a curve twice the length of *W* at the end of a word.

daily	tally	jolly	folly	follies	family	families

dairy	dairies	tarry	tarries	worry	worries	weary

Mary	marry	marries	valley	volley	volleys	valleys

factory	factories	battery	batteries	watery	flattery

Tory	Tories	story	diary	diaries	flurry	furry	airy

blue	blew	brew	crew	clot	clothing	calm	cram	claim

silly	hilly	daily	dallies	holy	doily	sally	alley

post	boast	lack	pest	best	beast	crest	ghost	jest

Unit 4
Speed Graphs

this

that

there

for (or)

have (or)

from (or)

son, sun

soon

very (or)

ever-y (or)

cover

regard

regret

regular

they

year

order

opinion

position

about

gave

practice-d
 practical

careful

summer

enough

sufficient

give-n

money

month

bill

become

immediate-ly

*learn

let-ter

name

newspaper

object-ion

our-hour

business

behind

character

---

*See page 55.

Speed Groups

may be	may have	may have been	is not	he is not-going

1.

2.

she is not	it is not	this is	this is not	that is not

1.

2.

I am not	is this	is that	is there	there is not-to be

1.

2.

for you	from you	have you	have you been	for the-good of

1.

2.

from the	we have	they have	I have	your letter-we

1.

2.

Unit 5

Sentences to Be Read and Practiced

DIRECTIONS: Read each sentence. Then, write it in your notebook three times. Read your notes aloud or silently. Then fill the blank spaces below.

1. *[shorthand outline]*

(a)

(b)

2. *[shorthand outline]*

(a)

(b)

3. *[shorthand outline]*

(a)

(b)

4. *[shorthand outline]*

(a)

(b)

5. *[shorthand outline]*

(a)

(b)

Sentences to Be Written and Practiced

(a) Have you seen my oxen? I saw your ox eating grass.

1.

2.

(b) Do not go to sleep on the fence; you might fall off.

1.

2.

(c) The high tax this year will vex our people.

1.

2.

(d) Do not seek a rear seat. I do not like a rear seat.

1.

2.

(e) I *swam a river of great size. Did you swim a river?

1.

2.

---

*SW ⟍ . See page 41.

(f) The fish has a fin and the bear has a pelt.

1.

2.

(g) *Ocean Grove has a camp meeting every summer.

1.

2.

(h) Will you go to the camp meeting in Ocean Grove this summer?

1.

2.

(i) I shall go if I have money enough to pay my way.

1.

2.

(j) How much money will it take to go for a month?

1.

2.

---

*Ocean *q* .

BRIEF SUMMARY REVIEW
of
LESSONS ONE, TWO, THREE

Dot and Circle Vowels: I E O OO

Four Consonant Curves: H W L R

Four Straight Consonants: T D N M

(Remember T and D are written downward.)

Four Blends: TH SH CH ST

Five Left Curves—Two *down* and three *up*

P B K G J

Angle and Hook Vowels: Angle A Hook A U Y

Diphthongs: OI-OY OU-OW

Left or Right Hook C ⊂ ⊃ Cross X x

Right *or* Left Downward Curves: S Z F V

Review Speed Graphs and Groups in these lessons.

Use Short L: (1) After horizontal strokes. still

(2) After downward left curves. apple

(3) To represent *LT* as the end of a word. fault

Practice again all the above fundamental characters.

Read again the shorthand sentences in Lessons One, Two, Three.

Write again the longhand sentences in shorthand.

Write in shorthand ten easy sentences of your own composition and read them aloud.

PRACTICE ON PLACE BLENDS
Superscript R—Subscript L

BL	blue	blur	bloat		*BR*	brag	·brick	brain
CL	class	close	clay		*CR*	cross	crease	crop
DR	drag	draw	drive		*TR*	trace	track	*tramp
FL	flail	flax	flue		*FR*	frail	freak	fritter
GL	glace	glare	glee		*GR*	grain	grate	grease
PL	plan	plea	place		*PR*	prim	prince	prize

SL	slate	slip	sleep	sledge	slave	slaw	sling

TEL tell telephone teller *REL* relation reel

VEL velvet vellum

Review pages 25 and 27.

Joe and John will go to the city to get a job in an airplane factory.

NOTE: *A* is generally understood between reverse curves.

pale	pear	pair	bale	bear	rag	lake	rage

*MP is *M* slanted downward. *SK* is a right curve a half longer than *R*.

EVANS SCIENTIFIC SPEED SHORTHAND
IS
BUILT AROUND THE CIRCLE

Lessons Four and Five are devoted to the study of Blends. But, before beginning their study it is well to observe that 80 per cent of the alphabetic characters are "built around the circle" so that they are easily formed and are, therefore, rapid to write. And, in addition they are most legible.

Of total strokes 80 per cent are circles, curves, hooks, and loops.

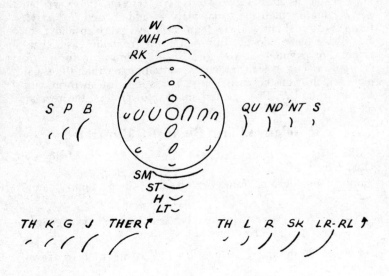

See pp. 100-101.

Importance of Blends

32. Blends shorten outlines, increase speed, and make reading easier. Hence, they should be carefully studied.

Blends consist of consonant combinations and vowel-consonant combinations spoken with a single or prolonged voice impulse. And, for convenience a few syllables are classed as blends although they are not pure blends.

ALL BLENDS ARE SINGLE PEN STROKES IN THE EVANS SPEED SYSTEM instead of two or more strokes as they are in other systems. See pages 39, 40, 41, 49, 100 , and 101 .

There are two general classes of blends: *Form* and *Place*. And, each general class consists of two kinds.

Form blends are: (a) *Original* — those not derived from other characters, and (b) *Relative* — those derived from or related to basic shorthand characters. About three-fourths of total Form blends are Relative.

Place blends are of two kinds: *Superscript*, those written slightly higher than the usual place to add *R*, and *Subscript*, those written slightly lower than the usual place to add *L* or *EL*. Place blends do not differ in form from the basic characters. For example, *B*, *BR*, and *BL* are identical in form. *BR* is simply *B* (the basic character) written higher than the usual place which is on the writing line. *BL* is identical in form with *B*. But to add *L*, *B* is written slightly lower than the regular place.

The Relative Form Blend MP Illustrated

33. *M* is a horizontal stroke like this ___ . *MP* is *M* slightly tilted like this ___ .

stamp lamp vamp ramp camp imp limp lump damp

NOTE: *PR* is the most frequently used blend in our language; *TH* is second, and *ST* is third.

Lessons Four and Five are devoted to the study of *form blends*.

How Original Blends Are Formed

34. As already stated blends shorten outlines and hence increase speed, and make reading easier. These facts will now be illustrated.

Take the word *straight*. In this system it is written with only two pen strokes as compared with five in another well-known system. The shorthand outlines compared: Evans ⌐⟋ ; the other ⟋⟋ . It is evident that two strokes can be read more quickly than five. Also, it is plain that two strokes can be written more quickly and easily than five.

As a blend occurs in every third word on the average, their value is evident.

We have already studied *Place Blends* (superscript to add *R* and subscript to add *L* or *EL*) in Lessons One, Two, and Three. Lessons Four and Five treat of Form Blends. Original Form Blends are single pen strokes arbitrarily devised for the purpose stated above.

Refer to Lesson Four, Unit 1.

TH is a short right or left curve written upward. Half the length of *K* or *L*. TH ⌒   K ⌒   TH ⌣   L ⌣ .

WH is twice as long as *W*. W ⌒   WH ⌒ . *RK* is three times as long as *W*. W ⌒   RK ⌒ .

NK, NG, and *NCH* are downward right curves as shown.

As *Q* is always followed by *U* the blend represents *QU* and not *Q* alone. It is a downward right curve the length of *B*.

RT is exactly like *H* but *H* is never sounded at the last of a word and *RT* occurs only at the terminal end of words.

Refer to Lesson Four, Unit 3.

ST is twice as long as *H*. *SM* is three times as long as *H*.

SH, SN, and *SW* are written as shown.

SK is three times as long as *L*. L ⟋   SK ⟋

SP is a large loop open at the bottom. ⟨⟩

How Relative Blends Are Formed

35. Relative blends are derived from and definitely related to the letters of the shorthand alphabet. They are expressed by:

(1) *Superscript,* which has been previously explained. (See pages 5, 26, and 34.)

(2) *Subscript,* which has also been explained previously. (See pages 24, 26 and 34.)

(3) *Joinings.* (Turn to Lesson Four, Unit 2.) *MEN-NEM-MEM* are *M* and *N* joined. *TED-DET-DED* are *T* and *D* joined.

(4) *Modified joinings. LR-RL* are *L* and *R* joined, but the angle between is disregarded so as to form a single continuous stroke.

(5) *Shortening. LT* is half the length of *H*.

(6) *Lengthening. THER* is the left curve for *TH* greatly lengthened.

(7) *Straightening. LD* and *RD* are *L* and *R* straightened.

(8) "Cutting corners" to form curves or semi-loops. (Turn to Lesson Five, Unit 1.) NT ⌐) "cutting the corner" ND⌐) TM ⌣ etc. *JENT* is *J* ⟋ and *NT*) joined ⌒).

CHART No. 7

Original Speed Blends

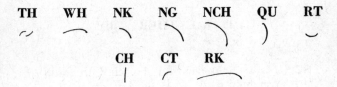

TH	WH	NK	NG	NCH	QU	RT

CH	CT	RK

Illustrative Words for Study and Practice

36. whack whine whim whale while wheel what

sank sang song sink sing cinch wink wing winch

queen queer quote quail quack quick quoth quite

port pert bort sort fort heart start cart court

edict depict evict *convict deject attract addict elect

work fork cork mark park bark jerk quirk stork ark

quire †require esquire quibble frequent equipment quiz

*K for "con," "com," "coun."
†R often represents the prefix "re."

NOTE: The blends *CH* and *TH* were studied on pages 4 and 22.

CHART No. 8

Relative Form Blends

MEN-MEM-NEM   TED-DET-ED   LR-RL   LD

LT   RD   THER   *MP

37. *L* is straightened and shortened to form *LD*. *RD* is straightened *R*. *LT* is short *L*.

men mention mental remain-remember member manage

did-date-debt-dead   today-data   details   determine

quarrel barrel curl rural earl Carl Charles marl

collar tailor sailor parlor seller cellar boiler

hold held bold gold weld field mould sold cold

pelt belt bolt colt melt quilt felt silt fault

bard cord beard hoard board heard word lard ward

guard garden guardian roared stored steered jeered

other another mother either neither weather whether

*MP is illustrated at bottom page 36.

40

CHART No. 9

Special S Blends

(Original)

ST	SM	SH	SN	SW	SK	SP

38. state stain staid east stool stone steam rest

smash smite smart smoke bosom blossom smith smell

show shine rash lash flash wash gash trash ash

(or)

snow snail snake snag raisin lesson reason snob

swain swam swim swear swish sweep sweat swill

skate skit skip skin skein scan scheme scratch

span spin spill speak spoke spool Spain spell

spice spite spire spirit split splice spleen spot

spring sprinkle sprain sprig spry sprawl sprout

41

Unit 4

Speed Graphs

ask

skill
　school

think

thank
　thing

which

when

where

what

system

succeed
　success

suggest
　suggestion

same

some

keep

response
　-ible
　-ibility

men

many

money

manner

quantity

quality

respect-ful-ly

duty

question

quarter

request

would

could   or

immediate
　immediately

until

remain
　remember

excellent
　excel

exercise

New Jersey

Thursday

obtain

always

catalog

look

character

Ohio

o'clock

opportunity

Christmas

Easter

Speed Groups

they *were   we were   these were   those were   which were

1.

2.

3.

these will   those will   those are   we will   they will

1.

2.

3.

of you-r   of all   all of   of us   of these   of those

1.

2.

3.

of which   to which   which is   which was   what will-be

1.

2.

3.

when are   where will   where are   they will be   he will

1.

---

*W represents "were" in a Speed Group—at the end.

Unit 5

Sentences to Be Read and Practiced

(a)

1.

2.

(b)

1.

2.

(c)

1.

2.

(d)

1.

2.

(e)

1.

2.

(f) ....

1.

2.

(g)

1.

2.

(h)

1.

2.

(i)

1.

2.

(j)

1.

2.

---

*to do
†about skate

Unit 6

Sentences to Be Written

(a) I think the state is about the size of New Jersey.

1.

2.

(b) Why did you not hand me the whip when I asked for it?

1.

2.

(c) The quality of this seed is excellent but there is only a small quantity.

1.

2.

(d) By a streak of good luck we obtained this excellent stock.

1.

2.

(e) Did you see my little steel stove? It is in the sink.

1.

2.

(f) Give me the brush and I will stain the thin lath.

1.

2.

(g) The boat did not sink for the seas were quelled.

1.

2.

(h) Will you have a twinge of pain if I sing?

1.

2.

(i) He hung his cap on a peg over the open fireplace.

1.

2.

(j) The boy will drive the cows home about dusk, will he not?

1.

2.

Letters for Reading and Practice

1.   2.

[shorthand characters]

1.

Dear Sir:

Your letter of September 9 asks for glass vases.
I can not get glass vases here like the one shown
in your catalog.

I have taken the liberty of making some
changes in your order, which I am shipping today
and which I hope will prove satisfactory.

If you do not sell all these vases within sixty
days, please ship them back at our expense.
                    Very truly yours,

2.

Dear Sir:

My classes have increased this month so that I
must have more desks to accommodate my pupils.
I can not seat them all in this crowded room.

Please see that I get these desks immediately.

I thank you for the favor.
                    Very truly yours,

---

*Hook *A* for "ac"; *K* for "com"; *dt* for "date."

CHART No. 10

Relative Blends

NT	ND	TN	DN	TM	DM	MT	MD

DF-DV-TF   JENT

Words for Practice

39. went wend tent sent send cent land fond fiend

saint sand ten tenth tense dense tennis tinsel

deny defy defense definite deface diffuse edifice

mint mind pint bind grind grant grand find lined

patent talent latent blind client· wind kind India

temper temperate tempo· tempter temptation temblor

temple madam freedom kingdom wisdom demise

standard lint lintel rind fender dandy dander

laundry sentry century gander founder slander

fender vaunt fountain foundry demeanor develop

entire entirely endless until defer demur demean

gentle gentile pageant cogent gentlemen gentleman

Unit 2

40. Intersected left curve *V* represents *"tive"* ⌐.

native   motive   suggestive   positive   restive   dative

Intersected right curve *V* represents *"sive"* (*"cive"*)

passive   massive   elusive   exclusive   conducive   conclusive

Unit 3

Speed Graphs

time		and, hand	
certain		assist-ant assistance	
certificate		business	
differ-ent difference		system	
between become		cause because	
difficult-y		capital-ol	
society		clear-ly	
deliver-y		character	
attention		typewriter	
tomorrow		correct correction	
ten		collect-ion	
intent		credit-or	
intend		confident-ence-ant	
individual		typist	
avenue			

Speed Groups

at any	at any time	some time	some time ago	to me

to meet	to miss	to know	to note	of the	of all	I go

all of	morning	first	firm	affirm	confirm	I can not

he can not	I am going	I may	I must	I must have-the

she will be	she will have	to the	at the	very well

will be	will have	would like	I would like to have

to keep	to pay	up-to-date	with me	with him-you

at this	at that	at this time-that time	does not

for them-us	I believe	is due	to receive	to send

each morning	every morning	this morning	yesterday-m

Your letter of the 10th inst. is received. *In reply

------

*Write *N* above the line to add *R*.

Unit 4

Sentences to Be Read and Practiced

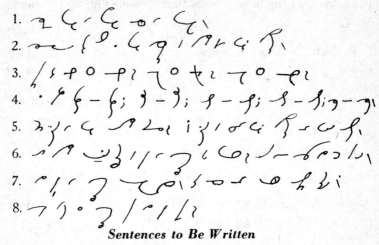

Sentences to Be Written

1. The timid boy could not estimate the cost of the patent.
2. Our tenant will pay his rent promptly and will not demur.
3. "My kingdom for a horse," the good king said.
4. You will enjoy greater freedom if you do not lose your temper.
5. He had the bond printed on a new brand of patent tinsel paper to bind the bargain.
6. Every teacher must have a certificate to teach school.
7. They delivered the merchandise by truck some time ago.
8. We need more space for our business which is now good.
9. Have you ever seen an airplane crash? I have not and I do not wish to hear or see a plane crash.
10. Mr. Smedley has a place of business where he sells evergreen trees at Christmas time.
11. I can not see you before the end of December, for this is our busy season.

timid   tenant   promptly   kingdom   bargain   merchandise

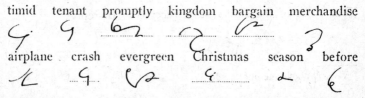

airplane   crash   evergreen   Christmas   season   before

Unit 5

Hints, Helps, and Suggestions

Abbreviations

41. Longhand abbreviations are frequently used in shorthand. The object is to secure shorter outlines.

company	department	general	January	railroad	dozen

42. IT IS PERMISSIBLE TO ABBREVIATE ANY LONG WORD by writing only enough to suggest the longhand.

possible	position	popular	success	magazine	problem

Expressing Negatives

43. Negatives are expressed by simple suggestive prefixes, sometimes by an initial vowel only.

Examples:	Positive	Negative
	material	immaterial
	moral	immoral
	necessary	unnecessary

When Vowels Occur Together

44. When two vowels occur together (and both are sounded) write them in their longhand order.

science	via	*radio	oriole	violin	iota	idea	lion

folio	area	piano	diet	riot	†cereal	†serial	create

prior	briar	friar	creation	aria	alias	(alas)	fiat

---

*I is written inside of the circle *O.* †*RL* blend.

Speed Graphs as Part of a Word

45. Speed Graphs frequently form an integral part of a longer word and must be given their Speed Graph value in transcribing.

goodness   welcome   willingness   advertisement   gladly

questionnaire   advantageous   *formality   greatness

46. A dot represents "thing" as a word ending. A superscript consonant may include *AR* or *ER*.

nothing   anything   hard   harp   star   starve   hermit   pardon

47. Intersections are often used to shorten outlines.

first class   way bill   price list   list price   p.m.

board of trade   cloak department   (D for department)

suit department   credit department   per cent   (a.m.)

48. *A* is understood between reverse curves.

band   brand   paint   plant   bland   waster   gale   jail

pail   bail   hark   lark   stark   lake   rake   rag   rage

49. "Sis" and "ses" are expressed by longhand *s*   .

masses   vases   roses   leases   molasses   †advises   rises

50. Use alphabetic *R* between two vowels.

erase   arise   oration   error   sorrow   derive   cabaret

---

*Detached for "ality."
†Hook for ad.

Omission of R After a Circle

51. *R* is frequently omitted after a circle but it must be supplied in the transcript to complete the word sense.

serve　　verse　　organ　　orbit　　orchard　　reverse　　converse

52. One who is often expressed by detached *R*.

reporter　debtor　　editor　　dealer　manufacturer　doubter

53. Indistinct *T* is frequently omitted.

expect　depict　predict　product　left　lift　rift　sift

54. *U* may express "ure" at the end of a word.

sure　assure　leisure　pressure　pleasure　insure-ance

nature　measure　furniture　feature　fissure　erasure

55. *U* is often omitted when it is clearly understood.

conclude　conclusion　preclude　result　insult　consult

56. At the end of a word *S* may represent "ous," "ious," and "eous."

gorgeous　glorious　fabulous　dubious　various　notorious

57. Care must be taken to write *I* plainly *superscript* to add *R*.

skit　skirt　thirty　thirsty　admission　admiration

C may represent "cy" at the end of a word: fancy

Unit 6

1.

Letters

2.

1.

Mr. James Phillips, Sidney, Ohio
Dear Sir:

I can not say that I am in favor of your scheme.
I am always against anything that means money
must be raised after the work is finished. I
think the money should be raised first, and then
you can see what can be done with the money you
have on hand.

Suppose we try to raise $5000 so as to get the
work started and then we can probably raise
another $5000 to help finish it.   Yours truly,

2.

Mr. Henry Dix, Shell Lake, Maine
Dear Sir:

I have seen Mr. Saxe and he says he is far too
busy to take over our work at this time. He is in
favor of fixing over the factory for next season.

Earl Rix may not be too busy. Shall I see him
about it so that the work may proceed without
loss of time? I am anxious to have this work go
forward without any further delay.

Very truly yours,

SHORTHAND VOCABULARY BUILDING

Memorize the shorthand outlines for the words on this page.

The 100 most-used words in the English language are given on this page (arranged in the order of frequency). As they, with their repetitions, comprise about three-fourths of the total words ordinarily used, the shorthand outlines for the words should be committed before proceeding further.

58.

the	and	of	to	*I	*a	in	that	you	for	it

was	is	will	as	have	not	with	be	your	at

we	on	he	by	but	my	this	his	which	dear

from	are	all	me	so	one	*if	they	had	has

very	were	been	would	she	or	there	her	an

when	time	go	some	any	can	what	send	out

them	him	more	no	about	please	week	night

their	other	up	our	good	say	could	who	may

letter	make	write	thing	think	should	truly

now	its	two	take	thank	do	after	than	sir

last	house	just	over	then	work	day	here

---

*I is written above the line; *a*, on the line; *if*, below the line.

SUGGESTIONS FOR FURTHER STUDY

1. Review lessons previously studied one at a time.

2. Study a section of the 1,000 most-used words on pages 72 to 86 of this manual.

3. Write in shorthand at least three times a page or more of the letters and articles in Lesson Six. Always READ what you write.

4. After completing the review of Lessons One to Five inclusive, study as many advance pages as you can master beginning with Lesson Seven and continuing through Lesson Ten. It is understood that you will continue Lesson Six with this advance work until it is completed.

LESSON SIX

Letters

1.   **2.**

[shorthand outlines]

1.

Dear Sir:

   We thank you for your quotation of May 26, but
we are not now in the market for lumber. A little
later, when business is a little better, we shall
be glad to have you write us again. We may then
be able to do business with you.

   If you have any special bargains at any time
we shall be glad to receive quotations with a
view to making immediate purchase as we are always
on the lookout for special bargain lots.

                    Very truly yours,

2.

Dear Mr. Jones:

   We received your quotation on a lot of lumber
which you wish to dispose of immediately. Your
price is satisfactory and I accept your offer.
You may ship via B & O to Zanesville, Ohio.

   We understand this lumber is first class and we
shall pay cash as soon as we have examined it so
as to get the benefit of your cash discount.

                    Yours truly,

May Takes a Position

May will take her new position today. Her work will be writing letters and orders. We believe she will do very well with this. May will have to get to the office early each morning. For a few mornings she may have to leave home before seven, and it is possible she may want to leave home before six so as to have everything in good order before her boss arrives.

The company has asked May to make a carbon copy of all letters and orders, and she will have to file *duplicate copies (carbon copies) of all letters she writes. She will also have to file all letters received so that she can find them quickly when asked to do so.

All correspondence should be ready as soon as she can get it out without making mistakes. May is thrilled at the prospect of a good position. She need not fear, for she is well prepared and she will do her best.

*Duplicate ⌐⌐⌐⌐

May Opens a Bank Account

It is now the end of the first week for May in her new position. She has received $50 and is very happy to get it, for this is the first money May has ever earned. She is now planning just what to do with her first earnings. Before she spends any of it she has decided to open a savings bank account. She will thus save a part of her salary each week. Perhaps she will join a Christmas club, so that when Christmas comes she will not have to disturb her savings.

The office manager has complimented May on her excellent work and she has decided to improve all she can for she has one eye on a salary increase which has been promised her if she makes good. If she gets this increase she can then save more money and have more to spend for clothing and sundry other articles which every girl needs.

May Is Promoted

May has received her first salary promotion. She has been in this office about three months. She has learned the office routine and now has many duties to perform which were not required of her in the beginning. For example, she now makes the bank deposits by first counting the cash and checks and listing them separately on the bank deposit slip—all of which she takes to the bank with the company's passbook. Arriving at the bank, she hands the currency, checks, deposit slip, and passbook to the receiving teller and he makes the proper entry for the amount deposited.

May now has charge of the files. When letters or orders are wanted she can find them quickly. She uses the adding machine and *mimeograph. She makes up the office payroll, and must make the proper entries for the social †security tax. May is now beginning to feel that she has started "up the ladder."

---

*Mimeograph ....   †Security ....

May Attends Evening School

In order to broaden her knowledge of the principles of business and to advance further in her present position or to get a better position, May has decided to attend evening school. She is taking the following subjects: Office Management, Corporation Finance, and Economics.

These advanced studies will broaden her outlook and give her a working knowledge of the *executive †functions of business administration. Although May does not expect to spend all her life in the office, she desires to get as good a position as possible while she is working.

She ‡will be able to write many business letters without dictation, compose them properly, punctuate and paragraph correctly. She may be called on to write reports of the directors' meetings, and she will certainly want to know how to use business reference books.

*Executive ....   †Function ....   ‡Will be able ....

Letter

Dear Miss Smith:

  You have asked us about night school. In
response to your inquiry we are inclosing a circular which gives general information about.
our evening school.

  If there are any questions you would like to
ask, please feel at perfect liberty to do so; we
shall gladly answer them.

  Night school is held on Monday and Thursday
evening from 7 to 9 o'clock. We shall be glad
to see you any time you may wish to enter. You
will find it somewhat to your advantage to enter
Monday, January 31, as this date is the beginning
of the winter term.

                    Very truly yours,

In re   In reply

In regard   In response

A   LETTERS   B

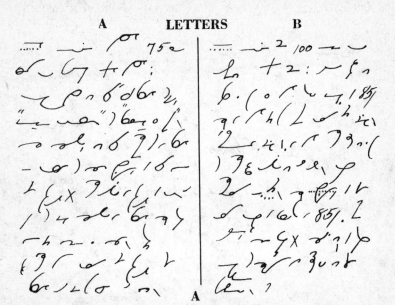

A

Mrs. Martin Jones, 75 East Orange Street, Baltimore, Maryland

Dear Mrs. Jones: Some time ago you ordered two books entitled, "American History," and "Poems of Today." When we received your order we did not have the books in stock, and were obliged to order them from the publisher.

We have written the publishers to hasten their delivery, and soon as we receive the books we shall forward them to you within a week.

Very truly yours,

B

Mr. Martin Crane, 100 Main Street, Rochester, N. Y.

Dear Mr. Crane: Last September you bought a bill of goods from us amounting to $85.00. We shipped the goods to you, but have not heard from you since. Every month since shipping the goods we have sent you a bill and we have also written you three letters. However, we have heard nothing from you. We shall be obliged to take legal steps to collect the $85.00 if you do not remit within ten days.

We think you wish to avoid embarrassment and we suggest that you send us your check by return mail.

Yours truly,

C

[shorthand notation]

D

[shorthand notation]

C

Miss Mary Peters, 205 North Avenue, Columbus, Ohio.
Dear Miss Peters: About a week ago we received
an order from you for 2 artists' smocks. Although
we placed an order for these goods with the manufacturer early in the spring, we have not received
any of the stock ordered, but we are daily
expecting the shipment to arrive.

We are therefore confident that we shall be
able to fill your order within the next few days.
Please pardon the unavoidable delay on our part.

Truly yours,

D

Pennsylvania Mining Co., Harrisburg,
Pennsylvania

Gentlemen: For the past several days we have had
trouble with some of our mining machinery. The
elevator in shaft No. 20 appears out of align-
ment so the cages sometimes stick and sometimes
they vibrate a great deal to the annoyance of
passengers. We have had the engine inspected
and have had the overhead gear repaired, but these
do not seem to remedy the trouble. Will you
please send an engineer to remedy the defect?

Very truly yours,

E

[shorthand notation]

F

[shorthand notation]

E

The Brown-Buick Automobile Co., 42 Mount Royal
  Avenue, Cincinnati, Ohio

Gentlemen: In another envelope we are sending
you enough proofs of the next truck advertisement
so that every truck man in your organization may
have a copy. We scarcely need to emphasize the
importance of keeping the organization in touch
with the National Packard Advertising, as advertising means more business and more business
should mean more profit to your company. Please
refer to your newspaper schedule for the exact
date of publication. Yours truly,

F

Northern Alabama Lumber Co., Birmingham,
  Ala.

Gentlemen: If you are in a position to quote on
the inclosed list of hard woods we shall thank
you to give us your very lowest prices delivered
on a Nashville, Tenn., rate of freight subject
to our commission of 5% and 2% for cash.

  If you do not have any of this stock on hand but
are in a position to cut and ship it in three or
four weeks, please write us. Yours truly,

G

H

G

Mr. Ralph H. Brooks, 45 Collins Street, Wheeling,
W. Va.

Dear Sir: We are informed by our factory that you
are in the market for a used Ford car, runabout
preferred. At present we have no used cars on
hand; but several of our owners are contemplating
turning in their cars on a trade and I have no
doubt that some one of these cars will be just
what you are looking for.

When any car comes in that I think will suit
you, I will telephone you. Yours truly,

H

Virginia Supply Co., Richmond,
Virginia

Gentlemen: We thank you for your letter of the
10th and note what you say in reference to furnish-
ing us some stock. It will be a pleasure to send
you our inquiries from time to time. At present
we should be glad to have you quote us on
hard wood mixed, as noted on the inclosed sheet.
Please quote us also on poplar or mixed hard wood
lath. Give us your best prices. Very truly
yours,

I

[shorthand notation]

J

[shorthand notation]

I

The Men's Shop, 208 Third Street, Lakewood,
  New Jersey

Gentlemen: We have finally succeeded in getting
the matter of George Jones's account settled in
full for the sum of $110.

The enclosed statement gives the accounting
in detail, showing the amount collected, the
sum advanced by you, our commission, and the
court costs. Our check for $78.15, covering the
balance due you is enclosed. Sincerely yours,

J

The Young Women's Shoppe, 444 Third Street,
  Springfield, Ohio

Gentlemen: I have the account of Mrs. Jane Smith
and have already given it my attention.

When I called Mrs. Smith on the telephone
today, I found that she is working part time.
She promised to commence paying the account just
as soon as she receives her first monthly salary
check.

I will keep in touch with her and will try to
get the payment started promptly. Yours very
truly,

K

[shorthand notation]

L

[shorthand notation]

K

Mr. John Brock, 110 Shady Boulevard, Portland,
　Oregon

Dear Mr. Brock: As we have received no answer
to our letter of October 22, we still do not
understand why we have not received a remittance
from you.

　We should like to have a payment on your bill
of June 18; but if for any reason you are not able
to pay the bill now, we will gladly extend the
time for you.　A remittance by return mail will
be greatly appreciated.　Very truly yours,

L

Mr. James Carr, 94 Terrace Place, Dover,
　Delaware

Dear Mr. Carr: We are returning your check,
number 943, for $15.34, which you sent in payment
of the merchandise you ordered February 10.

　This material was sent C.O.D., which is our
practice when mail orders are not accompanied
by a remittance.　As C.O.D. returns have already
been received, there is no charge against you
on our books.　Very truly yours,

M

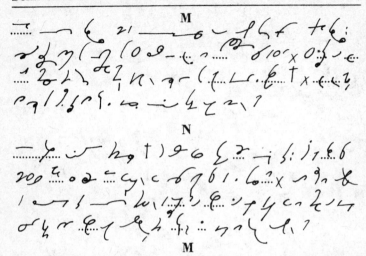

N

M

Mrs. Mary Beaver; 21 Monmouth Street, Red Bank,
　New Jersey

Dear Mrs. Beaver: We are very sorry that you
have been inconveniencd by our error in filling
your grocery order of the 10th.

　Our driver will call on Thursday afternoon
for the things you do not wish to keep. We shall
then be able to make a proper exchange.

　Please feel assured that we shall do everything to see that such an annoying mistake does
not happen again.

　　　　　　　　Yours truly,

N

Mr. Fred Hiram, Farmers Exchange & Loan
　Company, Battle Creek, Michigan
Dear Sir: I have at present about 20,000 acres
of corn land under cultivation. All weather
conditions point to a banner year.

　Will you send your representative to estimate
its market value? To harvest this crop I will
need $1,000. Can you advance this amount on the
surety that the crop can be reserved for your
purchase?

　I await your favorable reply.

　　　　　　　　Yours truly,

SHORTHAND VOCABULARY BUILDING

The shorthand outlines for the "1000 most-used words" are given below. They comprise about 96 per cent of the words most frequently used in speaking and writing. They are arranged in alphabetic order. Speed Graphs are in *italics* and should be memorized. It is recommended that they be learned by alphabetic sections as marked.

A

*a	able	aboard	*about*	*above*	absence	accept

accident	according	*account*	across	act	action	add

addition	address	adopt	affair	afraid	*after*	afternoon

again	*against*	age	ago	agreement	*air*	alike	*all*

allege	allow	*almost*	alone	*along*	*already*	also	although

always	am	*among*	*amount*	*an	*and*	annual	another

answer	*any*	anything	anyway	appear	application	*appoint*

appreciate	*April*	*are*	argument	army	around	*arrange*

arrangement	arrest	arrive	article	*as*	*ask*	assist

associate	*association*	assure	at	athletic	attempt	attend

attention	August	aunt	auto	automobile	avenue	await

away	awful

B

baby back bad ball band *be* bear beautiful became

because *become* bed *been* *before* beg began begin

beginning begun *behind* *believe* belong beside best

better between big *bill* black block blow blue

board boat *body* book born both bought box boy

bridge *bring* broke *brother* brought *build* *built* burn

business busy *but* buy *by*

C

call came camp *can* *cannot* capture *car* card *care*

career carried carry case cast catch *cause* celebration

cent center century *certain* chain *change* *character*

charge check chief *child* *children* *Christmas* church

circular circumstance cities citizen city claim class

clean *clear* clerk close clothing club cold *collect*

colonies combination *come* comfort *coming* command

committee common *company* complaint complete concern

condition conference connection *consider* *consideration* contain   convenient   convict   *copy*   cordially   cost   *could*

country   course   court   *cover*   crowd   cut

D

dark   dash   *date*   daughter   day   dead   deal   dear

death   debate   December   decide   decision   declare   deep

degree   delay   *department*   *desire*   destroy   develop

diamond   *did*   died   *difference*   *different*   *difficulty*   direct

direction   director   disappoint   discussion   distinguish

distribute   district   divide   *do*   *doctor*   does   *dollar*   done

don't   door   doubt   down   *dozen*   dress   driven   drown

due   *during*   duty

E

each   earliest   early   east   easy   eat   *education*   effect   effort

eight   either   elaborate   elect   election   *else*   emergency

empire   employ   *enclose*   end   engage   engine   enjoy

enough   *enter*   entertain   *entire*   entitle   entrance   escape

especially   estate   estimate   even   evening   event   *ever*

every   everything   evidence   examination   *except*   expect

expense   *experience*   *express*   *extra*   extreme   *eye*

F

face   fact   factory   fail   fair   fall   family   famous   far
(or)

farther   father   favor   feature   February   *feel*   feet

fell   felt   few   field   fifth   fight   figure   file   *fill*   final

finally   find   fine   finish   fire   *firm*   *first*   five   fix
(or)

flight   flower   folks·   follow   foot   *for*   foreign   forenoon
(or)

forget   *form*   fortune   forty   *forward*   found   four
(or)   *(or)*

fourth   free   Friday   friend   *from*   front   *full*   further
(or)

G

game   *gave*   general   *gentlemen*   get   getting   *girl*   *give*

glad   glass   go   *God*   goes   gold   gone   *good*   got

government   grand   grant   *great*   ground   guess   guest

H

had   half   *hand*   happen   happy   hard   *has*   hat   *have*
(or)

he   head   *hear*   heard   heart   height   held   help   *her*

here   herself   high   *him*   himself   *his*   history   hold
(or)

home   honor   *hope*   horse   hot   *hour*   house   how

however   human   hurt   *husband*

I

I   ice   *if*   illustrate   *immediate*   *importance-important*

impossible   imprison   *improvement*   *in*   include   *income*

increase   indeed   *inform*   *information*   injure   inside

inspect   instead   *intend*   *interest*   *into*   investigate

invitation   *is*   issue   *it*   itself

J

jail   January   *judge*   *judgment*   *July*   *June*   *just*   justice

K

keep   kill   kind   knew   know   known

L

lady   lake   land   large   last   late   law   lay   lead   *learn*

least   leave   led   ledge   left   length   less   lesson   *let*

letter   liberty   life   light   like   line   list   little   live

local   *long*   *look*   lose   loss   lost   lot   *love*   low

M

machine   madam   made   mail   majority   make   *man*

manner   *many*   March   marriage   material   matter   May

may   maybe   mayor   me   mean   meant   measure   meet

member   *men*   mention   mere   might   mile   mind   mine

minute   Miss   miss   Monday   *money*   *month*   *more*

morning *most* mother motion mountain *move* **Mr.**

Mrs. *much* must my

N

name national navy near nearly *necessary* need

neighbor neither *never* new news *newspaper* next

nice night nine no none noon nor north *not*

nothing November now *number*

O

object *objection* oblige obtain occupy *o'clock* October

of off offer *office* *official* often old omit on

once *one* only open *opinion* or order organization

organize other ought *our* out outside over own

P

page paid pair paper *part* *particular* party pass

past pay people *perfect* perhaps period person

personal picture piece place plan plant play

pleasant *please* pleasure *point* police political poor

popular population *position* *possible* post *pound* power

practical prefer preliminary prepare *present* *president*

press	pretty	price	primary	*principal*	*principle*	print

prison	private	probably	proceed	*progress*	promise

prompt	proper	property	prove	provide	provision

public	*publication*	*publish*	purpose	push	*put*

Q

question	quite	quill	queer

R

race	*railroad*	rain	raise	ran	rapid	rate	rather

reach	read	ready	real	really	reason	receipt	*receive*

recent	*recommend*	*recover*	red	*refer*	*reference*	refuse

regard	region	relative	relief	*remain*	*remember*	repair

reply	report	*represent*	*request*	*respectfully*	*responsible*

rest	restrain	result	retire	*return*	ride	right	ring

river	road	room	round	royal	*rule*	run	running

S

said	sail	salary	*same*	Saturday	saw	say	says

scene	*school*	sea	search	second	*secretary*	section

secure	see	seem	seen	select	senate	send	sent

separate	September	serious	*serve*	service	session	set
			(or)	(or)		

seven   *several*   *shall*   she   shed   *ship*   *short*   *should*

show   shut   sick   side   sight   since   *sincerely*   *sir*   sister

sit   six   size   slide   small   so   soap   soft   sold   *some*

something   sometimes   *son*   song   *soon*   sorry   south

speak   *special*   spell   spend   spent   spring   stamp   stand

start   state   *statement*   station   stay   steamer   still   stole

stone   stood   stop   stopped   story   *street*   struck   study

subject   *success*   *such*   *sudden*   suffer   *suggest*   suit

summer   summon   Sunday   supply   support   suppose

sure   surprise   *system*

T

table   take   talk   tax   teach   teacher   tell   *ten*   tenth

term   terrible   *testimony*   *than*   *thank*   *that*   *the*   theatre

their   *them*   themselves   *then*   *there*   *therefore*   these

they   *thing*   *think*   third   *this*   those   though   thought

three   through   throw   Thursday   thus   ticket   *time*

tire   *to*   *today*   *together*   told   *tomorrow*   tonight   *too took　top　total　toward　town　track　train　travel

treasurer　tree　trip　trouble　true　truly　*trust*　try

Tuesday　turn　*two

U

unable　uncle　*under*　understand　unfortunate　unless

until　up　*upon*　*us*　use　usual

V

vacation　various　*very*　vessel　victim　view　visit

(or)

visitor　volume　vote

W

wait　walk　want　war　warm　*was*　watch　water

way　we　wear　weather　Wednesday　week　weight

well　went　*were*　west　what　*when*　*where*　whether

which　while　white　*who*　whole　whom　whose　why

wife　*will*　wind　winter　wire　*wish*　*with*　*within*

without　witness　woman　women　wonder　*wonderful*

word　work　*world*　*worth*　*would*　wreck　write

written　wrote

Y

yard　year　yes　yesterday　yet　you　young　your

*Too and *two* are written in full ⌐.

Speed Graphs Not in Foregoing List

absent   acceptance   acknowledge   advertise   belief   beyond

body   caller   capital   capitol   catalog   certificate   clearly

collection   confidant   confidence   confident   congress

congressional   considerable   co-operate   co-operation

corporate   corporation   correct   correction   correspond

correspondence   credit   creditor   custom   customer   data

debt   deliver   delivery   differ   discount   educate   exact

excel   excellent   except   exercise   favorable   fully

gentleman   given   govern   guilt   guilty   hundred

ignorance   ignorant   immediately   improve   inclose

independence   independent   individual   influence   instance

instant   insurance   insure   invoice   jury   knowledge

magazine   market   merchandise   mistake   mistaken

nevertheless   opportunity   practice   privilege   probable

problem   purchase   quality   quantity   quarter   railway

record   regret   regular   satisfaction   satisfactory   satisfy

signature   sir (ser-sur)   skill   succeed   sufficient
    6 or ᴊ

suggestion   sun   surely   territory   thorough   thoroughly

thousand   throughout   till   touch   truth   typewriter   union

welcome

LESSON SEVEN

Unit 1

Speed Groups

59. you will   you are   you can-not   you may-not   see

you know   you would   we would   we could-not   we are

we are not   we will   we will not   we shall-not-be

we may-be   we may go   we shall go   I may be-may have

we inclose   we have   we have not   we have not been able

we wish   I wish   your account-is past due   we do-not

I do not   I am not able   I shall go with you to the theater

which will   which are   which *were   which is   which was

will you   are you   with you   with which   of which-this

to which   by which   to us   to the   to come   to go-give

to ask   to this   to that   do this   do that   to sell-buy

to receive   to let   have been   (has been   had been)

will be   will not be   to be   to have   to me   to meet

to know   to note   this is-not   that is-not   there is-not

---

*W may represent "were" in phrases.

Letters

Miss Lila Brown
  Columbus, Ohio

Dear Miss Brown:

   (Will you) consider a position (with this)
firm? (You have been) (very highly) recommended
(to us) (by the) principal (of your) school.
(In the past) (we have had) a number of competent
assistants (from this) school, (and we have
learned) that (we can) rely (on its) students
(to do) excellent work.

   (We are very) particular (about the) quality
(of our) work (and we desire) (to employ) only
persons (who have had) (first class) training
(and who have) a will to succeed in their work.

   If (you desire) (to consider) (this position),
please call for an interview Monday, October 10,
at 2 (p.m.)

                    Very truly yours,

(Dear Mr.) Jones:

   (In reply to your letter) (regarding the)
vacancy (in your office) (I shall be) (very glad)
(to accept) the position.

   (I am pleased) (to know) that my principal has
recommended me, and (I shall do) everything in
my power (to fulfill) his (and your) expectations.

   Our school term here ends in about three weeks
when (I shall be) ready (to go) (to work).   If
(in the meantime) (you need) (some one) perhaps
my friend, Miss Little, could substitute (for
me), as (I am anxious) (to complete) my schooling
(in order) (to be) fully prepared (for this
position).   (I hope) this arrangement (will be)
satisfactory (to you.)

                    Very truly yours,

Unit 2

Speed Groups

there is-not   of which   of you-r   of all   all - of - the

of this   of the   of that   of us   I can not   I had not

I do not believe   I could   I would   I will not   and the

into the   and you are   of his   as - to the   it is   is it

for the   from the   if you will-are   is not   is the

is this   is there   is his   is he   it will-be-have

for us-use-him   Dear Sir   Dear Mr.-Mrs.-madam

Dear Miss   five cents - per cent - dollars - thousand

five thousand dollars   F. O. B.   five hundred - dollars

B & O   five gallons - barrels - feet   U. S.   U. S. A.

can be   can not be   have you-been   it has not been

he had-been   he will be   they can-not   may be-have

million   billion   very well-much   should be-have

we can   and company   as soon as   as well as   as much as

it will have   he will have   I shall not be-have this

Letters

Mrs. J. C. Miller
325 South St.
Omaha, Nebraska

Dear Mrs. Miller:

In order that we may consider properly your recent application for an account, we request you to send us the names of firms or individuals with whom you have had credit dealings. Also, please inform us regarding the business connections of Mr. Miller.

We are enclosing a stamped envelope for your convenience in replying.

Very truly yours,

Dear Madam:

We are glad to send you samples of gingham as you request and hope you will be able to make a satisfactory selection.

In placing your order we suggest you make a second choice, in case your first choice is no longer in stock.

We appreciate your inquiry and wish to serve you to your entire satisfaction.

Yours very truly,

Mr. Philip Long
364 River Road
Hartford, Conn.

Dear Sir:

Mr. Black, our credit manager, has referred your letter to the Employment Office. If you will call at this office some morning between ten and twelve, we shall be glad to talk with you.

Please bring this letter with you.

Very truly yours,

LESSON EIGHT

Unit 1

Prefixes—Joined

NOTE: Prefixes and suffixes are arranged in columns. The first column states the longhand prefix or suffix. The second column has the shorthand outline for them. The third column gives word illustrations.

Illustrative Words

60.

Prefixes	*SS					
AC, AD	Hook	account	accept	adjust	advance	again
AG	A					
AL	all	almost	also	although	alder	almanac
AFTER	after	afternoon		afterward		aftermath
ANTA	NT	antagonize	antelope	antidote	anteroom	
ANTE						
ANTI						
CON, COM	K	cogwheel	concept	conceit	counsel	
CAN, COG						
COUN		compete	complete	candy	candle	concert
			or			
CONF	KF	confine	confess	confide	comfit	comfort
COMF						
EM, IM	M	emboss	impose	import	impute	embark
EN, IN	N	enable	ensign	intense	invite	engine
FOR,	F	forgive	forbear	forego	fortune	
FORE	or					
EX	X	expose	export	expert	expense	expect

*shorthand symbols.

86

SELF	Two S Curves Joined	selfsame selfish selfishness self-made
SUB	S (or)	subway sublime subscribe subsidy
SUP	SP	supply suppose support supress-preme
UN	U on its side	unable uneasy unpack unknown unless
SES, SIS		roses losses sister scissors sustain
SUS		suspect suspicion suspicious Moses

Unit 2

Prefixes—Disjoined
(Sometimes Joined)

61.

ATIC ETIC ITIC	K subscript	critic dramatic phonetic erratic poetic
CIRC CIRCU CIRCUM	C	circle circus circuit circumstances
		circular circulation circumference
DES DIS	S (or)	despot desolate desolation desperate
	(or)	disguise disgrace distress dispose
ENTER INTER INTRO	NT)	entertain entrance interpose interfere
		introduce interim interview enterprise
MULTI	MUL	multiply multitude multiple multifold

OVER	O ⌃	overcome overtake overlook overcoat
UNDER	UN ⌣	undergo understand underneath
		undertook underline underbrush
SUPER	SP ⌒	supervise supersede superman
		superintend-ent superpose superfine
TRANS	T /	transmit transact-ion transmission
		transit transform translate translation
		transfer transport transparent-verse
EXTRA	XT ✗	extra extreme exterior extraordinary
EXTER	✗	exterminate extradition extravagant
MAGNA MAGNE MAGNI	Mag	magnanimous magnet-ize magnificent
SHORT	SH	shorthand shortage shortly shorter
SHIP	/	shipwreck shipyard shipshape shorten

Unit 3

Sentences to Be Read

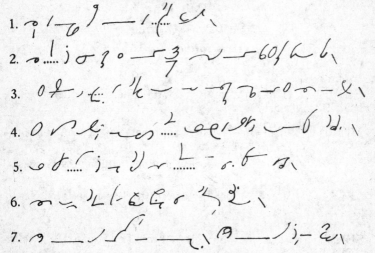

Sentences to Be Written

1. My overcoat was stolen at the circus by an underhanded thief who circulated among the crowd so that the police could not overtake him under the circumstances.

2. He was impressed by the fact that he could not get control of the very desirable government contract.

3. I understand that the ship owners accept a subsidy from the government.

4. Will you emboss the cards for me if I get an expert to supervise your work?

5. The counsel for the defense was almost ready to antagonize the judge but he endorsed the action of the lawyer for the plaintiff instead.

6. I anticipate that I shall not be incited to exert myself in order to do this work hastily and well.

7. Do not expect an unfailing supply to unfold from this parcel unless you have put a superabundance into it.

8. The note is overdue but he overlooked payment.

9. Can you transcribe the sentences to be read in this lesson? Bring your transcription to class.

10. James will translate his Latin but he cannot transport his baggage overseas.

Employ ⟋ or ⟍   Engaged ⟋   Agriculture ⟋ Retract

LESSON NINE

Unit 1

Suffixes—Joined

Illustrative Words

62.

Suffixes	*SS*	
FUL, FORE	F (or)	joyful awful therefore heretofore
MENT	M —	moment element experiment lament
NESS	N –	rudeness goodness willingness fastness
LESS	L , or ᴗ	unless useless tireless fireless wireless
SELF SELVES	Two S's ᴗ joined	himself herself yourself itself
		themselves ourselves yourselves
CTION,	KF ⌒	faction fiction fraction friction
CATION	⌒	diction location occasion occasionally
SION TION CIAN SHALL SHIP	SH |	nation notion motion session potion
		musician martial airship warship
		kinship partial credential
		steamship petition friendship worship
GATION	GF ⌒	legation litigation segregation
		mitigation congregation aggregation

90

Unit 2

Suffixes—Disjoined

63.

ACITY ICITY OSITY	S (or)	publicity sagacity veracity curiosity mendacity loquacity pugnacity
ALITY ELITY ILITY	L	fidelity virility gentility locality
ASTIC ESTIC ISTIC	ST	elastic artistic fantastic scholastic
BILITY BARITY	B	ability nobility barbarity liability
AVITY EVITY IVITY	V	levity brevity activity cavity nativity
FICATION	F	justification specification fortification
GRAM GRIM GRAPH	G	program pilgrim telegraph telegram
GRAPHY	GY	geography biography stenography
HOOD	OO O	manhood boyhood womanhood
WARD	D	eastward forward onward upward
ICAL ICLE	K	radical logical comical article mythical particle physical metaphysical fanatical

| OLOGY | O | apology | biology | analogy | geology |
| ALOGY | A | | | | |

| CIENT | F | patient | impatient | efficient | proficient |
| TIENT | | | | | |

| ULATE | UL | formulate | emulate | regulate | stimulate |

MENTAL	M	supplemental	ornamental	fundamental
		detrimental	experimental
		temperamental

| INGTON | TN | Lexington | Flemington | Arlington |

ARITY	R	charity	clarity	parity	verity	seniority
ERITY						
ORITY		authority		priority		minority

ANITY	N	vanity	sanity	serenity	divinity	unity
ENITY						
INITY						

AMITY	M T	calamity	extremity	dimity	femininity
EMITY					
IMITY					

| OLOGICAL | OJ | theological | psychological | physiological |
| | | technology | geological | biological |

Unit 3
Sentences to Be Read

1. [shorthand outline]
2. [shorthand outline]
3. [shorthand outline]
4. [shorthand outline]
5. [shorthand outline]
6. [shorthand outline]
7. [shorthand outline]
8. [shorthand outline]
9. [shorthand outline]
10. [shorthand outline]

Sentences to Be Written

1. His readings and writings were enjoyable.
2. An *icicle can not be mended.
3. Washington and Wellington were noted and noble men.
4. I took a teaspoonful of the medicine when I was lamed; therefore, I know the directions were readable.
5. My vacation will be possible only if I give diligent application to my duties during the next few months.
6. Did you study theology, psychology, or physiology?
7. Can you sing the doxology from memory?
8. His loquacity and mendacity led to much curiosity and publicity.
9. Will you go by steamship or airship?
10. Will you give me the specifications for the fortification?
11. He will formulate a program and telegraph it to his company which will compliment him for being efficient.
12. He had a cavity in his tooth.
13. I have a notion to use the lotion if you think there is sufficient justification.
14. His levity and brevity revealed his nativity.
15. This young lady has great ability in stenography.

---

*Icicle [shorthand outline]

Unit 4
Suggested Review of Prefixes and Suffixes
With Further Practice on Words Below

64.

accompany   or

adhere

agnostic

alderman

afterglow

antimony

cognovit

cancer

contrary

countersign

conference

comforter

emanate

impart

encircle

incarnate

forage

foretell

excite

self-reliance

suborn

supplant

unaware

sesame

sister-in-law

suspend

circumflex

destination

disagree

entrust

multigraph

overrule

underwrite

superabundant

transcend

extract

carefulness

doleful

armament

gladness

guileless

fractional

rotation

rapacity

personality

theology

bombastic

ancient

possibility

postulate

declivity

complemental

classification

Farmington

diagraph

priority

photography

insanity

childhood

typography

backward

sociology

technical

generality

1. He has a strong personality. Can you define personality? Is there a possibility of doing so?

2. There are many priorities during war times.

3. This young man majored in sociology during his college career.

4. Did you ever read ancient theology?

5. He has a bombastic disposition.

6. His reading is complemental to his studies.

7. There is no justification for a modification of our present plans.

8. This young lady had her photograph taken and then made a record on the phonograph to illustrate clearly the sound of the diagraph.

9. Can you describe the topography of Brazil?

10. Some sections of the country are very backward.

11. His vanity dates from childhood.

12. What is his draft classification?

LESSON TEN
Days, Months, States, Cities

Days

65. Sunday Monday Tuesday Wednesday Thursday Friday (or)

Saturday

Special Days

Good Friday   Easter   Fourth of July   Labor Day

Thanksgiving   Christmas

Months

66. January February March April May June July August

September October November December

States (Abbreviations)

67. Ala.   Ariz.   Ark.   Calif.   Colo.   Conn.   Del.   D.C.

Fla.   Ga.   Ida.   Ill.   Ind.   Ia.   Kans.   Ky.   La.   Maine   Md.

Mass.   Mich.   Minn.   Miss.   Mo.   Mont.   Nebr.   Nev.

N.H.   N.J.   N.M.   N.Y.   N.C.   N.Dak.   O.   Ore.   Pa.

R.I.   S.C.   S.Dak.   Tenn.   Tex.   Ut.   Vt.   Va.   Wis.   Wyo.

Principal Cities of the United States

Akron   Albany   Allentown   Atlanta   Baltimore   Bayonne

Birmingham   Boston   Bridgeport   Buffalo   Cambridge

Camden   Canton   Chicago   Cincinnati   Cleveland   Columbus
or

Dallas   Dayton   Denver   Des Moines   Detroit   Duluth

Elizabeth   El Paso   Erie   Evansville   Fall River   Flint
or

Fort Wayne   Fort Worth   Grand Rapids   Harrisburg

Hartford   Houston   Indianapolis   Jacksonville   Jersey City

Kansas City   Knoxville   Lawrence   Los Angeles   Louisville

Lowell   Lynn   Manchester   Memphis   Milwaukee   Minneapolis

Nashville   Newark   New Bedford   New Haven   New Orleans

New York   Norfolk   Oakland   Oklahoma City   Omaha   Paterson

Peoria   Philadelphia   Pittsburgh   Portland   Providence

Reading   Richmond   Rochester   St. Joseph   St. Louis

St. Paul   Salt Lake City   San Antonio   San Diego

San Francisco   Savannah   Schenectady   Scranton   Seattle

Sioux City   Somerville   South Bend   Spokane   Springfield

Syracuse   Tacoma   Toledo   Trenton   Troy   Tulsa   Utica

Washington   Waterbury   Wichita   Wilkes-Barre   Wilmington

Worcester   Yonkers   Youngstown

Canadian Provinces and Cities

Prince Edward Island   Nova Scotia   New Brunswick   Quebec

Ontario   Manitoba   Saskatchewan   Alberta   British Columbia

Yukon   N. W. Territory   Brantford   Newfoundland   Calgary

Edmonton   Hamilton   London   Montreal   Ottawa   Peterborough

Regina   St. John   Saskatoon   Toronto   Vancouver   Victoria

Windsor   Winnipeg   St. Johns   Grand Manan Island

Continents

North America   South America   Europe   Asia   Africa

Australia

Travel Article

Mr. and Mrs. James White left their home in Albany, New York, Saturday morning, June 7, for a tour through the Southern states of Virginia, North Carolina, South Carolina, Georgia, Florida, Alabama, Mississippi, and Louisiana. They traveled by boat from Albany to New York City, where they boarded a train for Washington, D. C.

At Washington they took the Southern railway for Miami, Florida, although they made short stops in Richmond, Virginia; and Raleigh, North Carolina. They would have liked to visit Wilmington, N. C., and Charleston, S. C.; but their schedule did not permit them to do so.

On their way to Los Angeles, California, they may fly from Miami to Atlanta, and from there to New Orleans. From New Orleans they will probably fly to Albuquerque, N. M., and then on to Los Angeles.

They will want to visit Pasadena and other interesting cities in Southern California.

Perhaps they will take a Southern Pacific train to San Francisco and Oakland. They will visit the Golden Gate Park while in San Francisco—perhaps on Monday, Tuesday, Wednesday, and Thursday for there is much to see in the Bay Cities. They will then go to Sacramento; Portland; Oregon; and Seattle, Washington.

From Seattle they will take the Northern Pacific to Spokane, and then drop down to Boise, Idaho.

On their return trip they will pass through Helena, Montana; St. Paul and Minneapolis, Minnesota; Milwaukee, Wisconsin; Chicago, Illinois; Indianapolis, Indiana; and Columbus, Ohio. And they may stop off in Buffalo, Rochester, and Syracuse, New York, on the latter part of the long journey.

Another interesting trip would be through the New England States of Massachusetts, with a visit at Boston, through Maine stopping at Portland and Augusta. At Eastport, Maine, they might take a boat over to Grand Manan Island, which is in the Bay of Fundy.

There are many interesting places in Vermont, New Hampshire, and Connecticut also.

Form Blends—*Original*

TH	WH	NK	NG	NCH	QU	CH	RT

Special S Blends—*Original*

ST	SM	SH	SN	SW	SK	SP

Form Blends—*Relative*

Curves

NT	ND	LT	LY	RY	RK	LR-RL	TH(E)R

Semi-loops

TN	DN	TM	DM	MT	MD	DF-DV-TF	JENT

Straight Lines

MEN-MEM-NEM	TED-DET-DED	LD	RD	MP

Place Blends—*Relative*

Superscript to Add R

TR	DR	PR	BR	KR	GR	FR	CR
/	/	(	(	⌐	⌐	\ or /	⌐ or ⌐

Blends Written Superscript to Add R

STR	SKR	THR	SPR	SHR	NTR
⌣	⌣	⌐ or ⌣	⌒			)

Subscript to Add L

PL	BL	KL	GL	FL	SL	CL
(	(	⌐	⌐	(or /	(or (	(or)

Straight Lines Subscript to Add EL

TEL	DEL	SHEL	SWEL
/	/	—|—	\

Two Blends Subscript to Add L

DFL	SPL
⊂	⌒

Two Curves Subscript to Add EL

VEL	REL
(	/

KEY TO EXERCISES

LESSON ONE

Unit Six

(Page 11) Sentences to Be Read and Practiced

(a) Don will row on the high tide. Will you row on the high tide with me?

(b) I will meet the hero here in a moment. Will you meet the hero?

(c) Helen will meet me in the hotel. I will meet Helen in the hotel.

(d) Ellen will need the needle. Will you need a needle? I shall need a needle.

(Page 12) Sentences to Be Written

(a)

(b)

(c)

(d)

(e)

SUGGESTION TO STUDENTS

Write each of the above sentences three times in shorthand and read every sentence each time you write it. Practice several times any outlines that give you trouble.

Do this with the following lessons also.

LESSON TWO

Unit Five

(Page 19) Sentences to Be Read and Practiced

(a) The dime is mine. Can you use the dime if I give it to you?

(b) Please give me a clean plate to put the good bread on.

(c) Will you wait till I bake the bread? It will be good bread.

(d) The little lad has had his bread and milk and will now lie down.

(e) The good judge will give the jury a special charge.

(f) Do you hear the hum of the lute? I like to hear the hum of the lute on a clear night.

(g) Are you going to take Helen home in the car?

(Pages 20-21) Sentences to Be Written

(a)

(b)

(c)

(d)

(e)

(f)

(g)

(h)

(i)

(j)

LESSON THREE
Unit Five
(Page 30) Sentences to Be Read and Practiced

(a) He will take his fiddle and play a lively tune for us.

(b) She will go to the creek with him to fish but she will not fib about the fish she catches.

(c) I will write you a letter and I shall expect to hear from you soon.

(d) Did you sell a sea shell or did you catch a fish by the gill?

(e) We have a rag rug on the floor behind the door.

(Pages 31-32) Sentences to Be Written

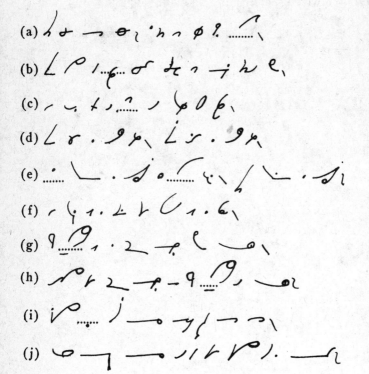

LESSON FOUR   **Unit Five**

(Pages 44-45) Sentences to Be Read and Practiced

(a) What will be their rank in the cast?

(b) Where are the men who were on duty?

(c) The dance which will be held on Thursday night will stop at 12 o'clock.

(d) I think our visitors will remain the rest of this month.

(e) When and where will you stock the stream with fish?

(f) Where were you while the whale was in sight?

(g) Do you remember the quota of money we had to raise?

(h) The water will quench his thirst, and if there is enough of it, it will also quench the fire.

(i) We would thank you to do immediately the thing I spoke to you about.

(j) Can you skate? I will go to the rink with you and try.

(Pages 46-47) Sentences to Be Written

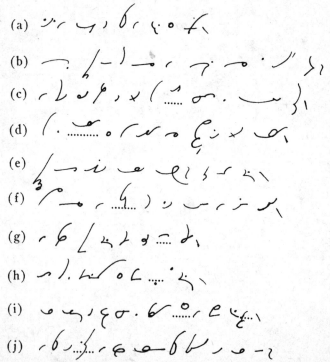

(a)

(b)

(c)

(d)

(e)

(f)

(g)

(h)

(i)

(j)

LESSON FIVE

Unit Four

(Page 52) Sentences to Be Read and Practiced

1. We shall not deface the edifice nor the temple.
2. We must pass through a dense woods to get to the tennis grounds.
3. Did you say notion or motion? knave or native? map or mop?
4. I said bent not bend, sent not send, lent not lend, rent not rend, went not wend.
5. Can you find the tennis racket for me? I shall find it on the tennis grounds in the tenth round.
6. Will you get Smith & Co. to deliver the merchandise to us tomorrow?
7. They delivered the merchandise some time ago; it is now in the store ready for sale.
8. What kind of merchandise did they deliver today?

Sentences to Be Written

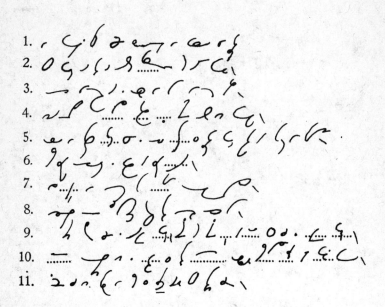

LESSON SEVEN (Page 83) Letters

[shorthand notation]

[shorthand notation]

(Page 85) Letters

[shorthand notation]

LESSON EIGHT

Unit Three

(Page 89) Sentences to Be Read and Practiced

1. We wish to employ several men to distribute the circulars.
2. We charge interest on accounts of more than $300 which are more than sixty days past due.
3. Our office manager is planning to introduce some new methods which should make our work more efficient.
4. Our agent received instruction from the home office to retract his statement about interfering.
5. He took great interest in his interview with the chairman of the appointment committee.
6. We were highly entertained by the expert opinions of the distinguished scientist.
7. These men are engaged in manufacturing. Those men are interested in agriculture.

Sentences to Be Written

1.
2.
3.
4.
5.
6.
7.
8.
9.
10.

LESSON NINE
Unit Three
(Page 93) Sentences to Be Read and Practiced

1. It was an enjoyable occasion. Occasionally we enjoy a musical.
2. You may gain more by being patient than by exercising impatience.
3. His fidelity and gentility led to his promotion by the officers of the corporation.
4. In worship and in friendship manhood and womanhood move onward toward atonement.
5. His prosperity enabled him to give much to his church and his lodge. Do you give much to your church or lodge or both?
6. Was there a good congregation at church this morning?
7. We cannot ride to business now, for our tires are worn out.
8. Did you ever attend a musical comedy?
9. Can you sing the doxology from memory?
10. Unless you can read and write these sentences readily, you had better review them.

Sentences to Be Written

LESSON NINE (continued)

9.

10.

11.

12.

13.

14.

15.

(Page 95) Review Sentences

1.

2.

3.

4.

5.

6.

7.

8.

9.

10.

11.

12.

LESSON TEN
(Page 99) Travel Article